Write Your Book:
A 30-Day Writing Guide to
Sharing Your Story with the World

Write Your Book:
A 30-Day Writing Guide to Sharing Your Story with the World

Var Kelly

Write Your Book:
A 30-Day Writing Guide to Sharing Your Story with the World

Just Write It Services (JWIS), LLC
Email: Info@JustWriteItServices.com
Website: www.JustWriteItServices.com

Other Books by Var Kelly

The Faith Reaction

My Family

Spiritual Renewal for Greater

The Art of Finishing

Write Your Book – Write Your Life Story

DEDICATION

To the one who faced insurmountable challenges—whether it was abuse, addiction, sickness, disease, or the curveballs life threw your way—this book is for you.

I dedicate this work to the fighter within you, the part of you that refused to let circumstances define your story. To the one who made the commitment to rise above the circumstances and situations, no matter who was at fault or what was to blame. You didn't let the pain, the setbacks, or the struggles keep you down. Instead, you chose to overcome.

You are no longer a victim—you are the victor. You've embraced the strength it takes to share your story, not just with friends, family, or those you inspire, but with the entire world. This book is a testament to your resilience, your courage, and your unwavering determination to turn your trials into triumphs.

This book is dedicated to you because you dared to believe that your voice matters and your story deserves to be told.

ACKNOWLEDGMENTS

First and foremost, I give all honor and thanks to God, The Father, Jesus Christ, The Son, and The Holy Spirit. Thank You for entrusting me with the ability to write. There was a time when I didn't know I had this gift, but over the years, You revealed it to me, nurtured it within me, and showed me how to use it. Not only have You given me the ability to write, but You've also blessed me with the opportunity to help others write as well. For this, I am eternally grateful.

To my dad and mom—the late Pastor Ivory Kelly and Lady Mary Kelly—I honor you by including the titles 'Pastor' and 'Lady' because they reflect the lives of faith, love, and leadership you have exemplified. I also call you dad and mom because you've been just that – a dad and mom.

- Dad, though you are no longer here, your legacy of faith and strength pushes me forward.
- Mom, you remain a steadfast spiritual example of unwavering faith in Christ and a source of encouragement.

Together, you gave me the space and freedom to follow God's leading in my life, and your support has meant more than words can express. Thank you for modeling a life of faith, encouraging me in my gifts, and always standing by my side.

TABLE OF CONTENTS

INTRODUCTION

Welcome to your 30-day writing challenge—a transformative journey that will take you from the dream of writing a book to holding a completed manuscript in your hands.

As a professional writing coach who has had the privilege of helping countless aspiring authors overcome self-doubt and lack of skills and finally deal with the uncertainty of writing and publishing their books, I've gathered years of experience while writing my books or helping others. All of this experience helped me to create a system that works. Thus, I have specifically designed this guided plan with you in mind.

This challenge is not just another writing guide; it's a structured, intentional plan crafted to walk you through writing a book step by step. Each day presents a specific action or task to complete, designed to help you stay on track and make measurable progress. These activities, which generally take between 30 minutes to 2 hours a day, ensure that you will have a completed manuscript by the end of 30 days.

Here's the exciting part: While this plan is designed to help you fast-track your writing process, it's also flexible. If life happens or you find yourself needing more time, you can adjust the pace. However, the purpose of this 30-day structure is to help you get the content for your book out of your head and onto the pages as quickly and efficiently as possible.

Let's face it—you've likely been carrying the desire to write your book for years, but for one reason or another, you haven't been able to turn that desire into action. Maybe you've been overwhelmed by the process, unsure of where to start, or plagued by thoughts of "I'm not a writer." That ends here. This challenge has been prepared with you in mind, offering a manageable and achievable roadmap to finally bring your story to life.

As you embark on this journey, I encourage you to commit fully. Each task builds on the last, and the momentum you create will carry you to the finish line.

Writing a book is not just about putting words on a page—it's about sharing your voice, your experiences, and your truth with the world. This 30-day plan will help you do just that.

This moment is your moment. Your story matters, and the world needs to read it. So, take a deep breath, make the commitment, and let's get started. By the end of these 30 days, you'll have achieved what once seemed impossible.

It's time to *"Write Your Book."*

BEFORE YOU START

Starting this 30-day writing journey requires preparation—not just mentally but also in how you set up your environment, manage your time, and equip yourself with the right tools. The foundation of your success lies in how well you plan your approach before you begin. In this section, we'll cover the essential elements you need to organize for the challenge.

Space

Each day, you'll need a dedicated space that supports your focus and creativity. This space should be free from distractions and external interactions, particularly from your cellphone or social media. Consider choosing a spot that feels inspiring yet comfortable—a desk by a window, a quiet corner, or even a local library.

Think of this space as your writing sanctuary. It's where you'll transform your thoughts into words, so treat it with the respect it deserves. Keep your tools organized, your distractions minimal, and your purpose clear.

Same Time Every Day

Consistency is key to completing this challenge. Carve out at least one hour each day at the same time to focus solely on your writing tasks. While some days may require more time, this dedicated hour is your minimum commitment. Always keep that hour's time slot as your writing time, no matter what. If you find you need additional time, still maintain your hour, but break up the rest of the necessary time into manageable chunks, like 30-minute or 15-minute increments, throughout your day.

Treat your writing time like a work shift. Just as you show up on time for a job, show up on time for yourself. If your writing hour is set for 8:00 AM, begin preparing by 7:50 AM so that you're ready to dive in when the clock strikes 8:00 AM.

Here's another point: While you treat your writing time like a work shift, don't consider writing your book as work. This is a book you've long desired to write. This book is your heart written on pages. It's your mind written for others to comprehend. It's your soul of emotions connecting with others. Writing your book isn't work, but it's a book of life and lessons.

Commit the time daily. Keep your schedule. It will be the driving force behind your success. So, meet up with yourself to write at the same time every day.

Computer Device

This 30-day challenge is designed with the assumption that you'll be using a computer device, such as a laptop or desktop, equipped with software like Microsoft Word or Google Docs. Having basic knowledge of using such tools—including saving documents, retrieving them, and utilizing features like copy, paste, and formatting—will streamline your writing process.

Using electronic documentation tools is highly recommended for several reasons:

1. Efficiency: Typing is faster than writing by hand, helping you meet daily word count goals.

2. Organization: Electronic files allow you to organize chapters, notes, and revisions seamlessly.

3. Backup: Your work can be saved and stored safely in the cloud or on external devices, ensuring it's never lost.

4. Editing Ease: Revising digital text is more efficient, with tools to track changes and refine grammar or structure.

While this 30-plan is ideal for electronic documentation, you can still participate using pen and paper if needed. However, be mindful that manual writing may require additional time to complete the daily tasks.

What Will Happen Each Day

Every day of this challenge has been carefully structured to help you build momentum and stay on track. Here's how each day is laid out:

*   Goal: Each day's task begins with a specific goal to keep your focus clear. This goal serves as the day's destination, guiding your efforts and ensuring progress.

- Time Commitment: To help you plan, each task includes an estimated time commitment, typically between 30 minutes to 2 hours.

- Prompts: Writing prompts are provided to spark ideas, focus your thoughts, and ensure you're covering essential aspects of your story.

- Expected Results: Most of the daily tasks outline what you should achieve by the end of the day. This gives you measurable outcomes and a sense of accomplishment.

Do You Really Want This?

Before you dive into this 30-day writing journey, take a moment to pause and ask yourself a critical question: *Do I really want this?*

What do I mean by *this* question? Do you truly have the passion and drive to write your book, or is it just a passing thought or competitive whim? Writing a book isn't just a fleeting idea—it requires intention, commitment, and heart. For many, the desire to write stems from a place of grit and reality. It comes from a deep need to share their truth and help others through their story. If that's you, then know this: just as you've faced challenges in life and moved from being a victim to a victor, you'll need to channel that same determination here.

This journey will ask you to show up for yourself every day. Writing a book isn't about picking through it and dabbling with it; it's about daily commitment to the tasks at hand. There will be days when doubt creeps in, and other days when emotional blocks pop-up. But just as you've pushed through adversity before, you must dig deep, move forward, and stay the course—

even when you don't fully understand the process.

Think about a moment in your life when you were ready to give up. Recall how you felt on the brink of quitting, yet somehow, the next day, you found the strength to move forward—and eventually found victory. That's the mindset you need for this 30-day writing plan. Push past confusion. Push past discomfort. Push past fear.

This plan is designed to help you move forward, step by step, even on the hardest days. Show up daily. Do the work. Focus on what makes sense and what feels right, and trust the process. Your story is uniquely yours, and your writing style doesn't need to mimic anyone else's. As you tackle the daily tasks, follow the guidance provided. Also, allow yourself to flow naturally with your voice and truth.

Your commitment will make all the difference. If you truly want this, if you're ready to honor your story and bring it to life, then the only thing left to do is show up. Do the work today, and then show up again tomorrow. Your determination and passion will carry you to the finish line. If you really want this, you *will* make it happen.

Prepare yourself, stay committed, and trust in the process. Your story is ready to be written, and this challenge will guide you every step of the way.

The Foundation Days (Days 1–7)

Who doesn't love stepping into a completed dream home? Imagine walking into a house where the walls are painted in your favorite colors, the furniture is perfectly arranged, and every detail—from the fixtures to the accents—reflects your vision. It's breathtaking, isn't it? Yet, it's easy to overlook the vital process that made that dream possible: the construction of the foundation.

The foundation of any home is what ensures its strength and durability. It's the hidden work beneath the surface—the digging, leveling, and securing—that allows the house to stand firm against time and the elements. Without a strong foundation, no amount of customization or decor can protect the house from eventual collapse.

The first seven days of this 30-day journey are all about laying the foundation for your book. Think of this week as the groundwork for your story, where you dig deep into your life experiences, your themes, and your purpose. These daily activities may feel simple or even unnecessary at times, but they are anything but. Each task is intentionally designed to give you clarity, direction, and stability as you move forward.

Building this foundation ensures that when the real work of writing begins, you'll have the strength to push through challenges like emotional blocks—those moments when the weight of your story feels too heavy—or writer's block, when the words simply won't come. With a solid foundation, you'll have the tools and focus to overcome these obstacles.

Think of your foundation as the blueprint. Thus, the notes and insights you generate during this time will become your anchor throughout the process. You can return to this foundation for inspiration, encouragement, and clarity whenever you feel overwhelmed or uncertain.

So, embrace this week of preparation. Lay the groundwork that will support your story, ensure its stability, and carry you through the writing process. Just as a well-built foundation ensures the strength of a home, your efforts this week will set the stage for a book that speaks to the hearts of your readers.

DAY 1

GOAL: Define Your Why?

As you start your writing journey, it's essential to understand your 'why.' Your 'why' is the heartbeat of your story, the very reason you've waited and longed to write this book for so long. Today's activity will help you capture your 'why,' which will serve as a daily reminder and guide throughout this 30-day process.

Read through the prompts and take a moment to reflect. Then, on your computer (or in your notebook), write your responses to each prompt. It's often helpful to create a list, as you may have multiple 'whys' connected to your story. After writing your list, spend another 10 minutes visualizing the person (real or imagined) you want to reach with this book. Picture their face, consider their life, their struggles, and their victories. Then, revisit your 'whys' to ensure that they resonate with the person you're writing for and connect with their journey.

When you're confident your 'whys' are aligned with your audience, save your notes, and if needed, rewrite or refine them as you go.

Make sure each reason is clear and speaks directly to the heart of the person you are writing to.

TIME COMMITMENT

30 minutes to 60 minutes

PROMPTS

- Why do you want to tell your life story?

- What impact do you hope it will have on others?

- What message or lesson is most important for you to share?

- In what ways could telling your story bring healing or closure to your life and to the life of the readers?

EXPECTED RESULTS

- A clear, personal motivation for writing.

- A deeper understanding of who you're writing for and why they need your story.

- A solid foundation for staying motivated and connected to your purpose during this journey.

- A clear picture of how sharing your story can make a difference in both your life and the lives of others.

"Your story holds the power to inspire, heal, and connect with someone who needs it most. Let your 'why' be the light that guides each word you write."

DAY 2

GOAL: Set The Tone

Today, you'll set the tone for your memoir, a key step in defining the personality and atmosphere of your writing. Whether your book is inspirational, humorous, or serious, this step ensures your memoir feels authentic and invites readers to connect with your unique voice.

Think about how you naturally express yourself in conversation—is it playful, reflective, or straightforward? Consider the person you're writing to, whether real or imagined. How would you share your life story with them? Let yourself explore the personality and energy you want to convey through your words.

Your tone and style represent how you write – how you communicate and share your authentic self. Your tone and style might be friendly, formal, conversational, emotional, philosophical, informative, candid, reflective, or somewhere in between. You have to consider how you communicate and use that as a guide to how you will write.

Some parts of your story may be dark and difficult to share, while others may be light and funny. Regardless of the content, your tone and style should remain consistent.

After some time reflecting on your tone and style, work through the prompts below and write your responses.

TIME COMMITMENT

30 minutes to 60 minutes

PROMPTS

- What kind of atmosphere do you want your readers to feel when they read your story (hopeful, humorous, introspective)?

- Think of a few words that describe your personality (e.g., warm, resilient, straightforward). How can you integrate this tone into your writing?

- Write a paragraph of one account you plan to write in your book. Then, re-read it and edit it. Does the tone fit your personality and how you want to share? Does this tone connect with the person you're writing to (real or imagined)?

EXPECTED RESULTS

- A clear sense of the tone and personality of your memoir.

- An understanding of how your unique voice can shape your story's impact.

- Confidence in writing authentically, letting readers experience your genuine self.

- A foundational element that brings cohesion to your chapters.

"Your story's power lies in its authenticity; let your tone reflect the truth of who you are, inviting readers to connect with the real you."

DAY 3

GOAL: Define Your Audience

For the past two days, you've been asked to visualize the person you're writing to—whether they are real, imagined, or even a representation of your younger self. Today, you'll continue visualizing this person to identify specific details about who they are and what they need. While your book will reach a broad audience, focusing on this one person will help you connect deeply with readers who share similar qualities or challenges.

By narrowing your focus to this "one person," you'll create a personal, authentic, and impactful manuscript for anyone who picks up your book. So, think about this individual. Take time today to visualize this person. Close your eyes and see them clearly. Think about their struggles, hopes, fears, and desires. Are they someone you know, or do they reflect a part of who you are? Imagine how your book might inspire, uplift, or provide clarity to them.

Write down what comes to mind—their personality, challenges, and what they're searching for in your book.

Keep this image of your ideal reader close as you continue your writing journey. Let them guide your words, ensuring your message stays personal and relatable. This focus will not only ground your writing but also create a connection that resonates with every reader who sees themselves in your story.

TIME COMMITMENT

45 minutes to 60 minutes

PROMPTS

- Who is the one person you would love to share your story with, and why? How old are they? Where do they live? Are they single, married or divorced? Do they have kids? What type of work do they do?

- Describe their life, challenges, and values. What themes or principles come to mind when you understand their challenges and values?

- What message would you want them to take away after reading your book?

- Imagine a conversation with this person. What would you say to encourage them, and how would you approach it? Write at least 3 paragraphs of what you would say.

EXPECTED RESULTS

- A detailed description of your "one person" audience.

- A focused sense of who you're writing to, which will help guide your tone and style.

- Clarity and confidence on the impact you hope your story will have on readers who identify with this individual.

"Speak to the heart of one, and you'll reach the souls of many. Let your words connect with the person who needs your story the most."

DAY 4

GOAL: Create Your Life Timeline

Today, you'll start building a timeline of your life's key events and milestones. This exercise will help you organize important moments chronologically, allowing you to reflect on experiences that shaped you. Remember, not every event on this list will necessarily make it into your book. Instead, think of this as gathering the raw material to support and build the foundation of your book and book's outline.

As many people often struggle with organizing their book's content, this exercise allows you to write it out, see it on paper, and assess the experiences you want in your book. Participating in this activity will help you release the memories from your mind onto paper. You will finally be able to begin to organize your thoughts.

As you see your life unfolding in chronological order, you'll gain a deeper understanding of how each experience contributed to your journey.

Trust the process—you're building the foundation that will support and guide your writing.

TIME COMMITMENT

45 minutes to 60 minutes

PROMPTS

- Start by listing 10 to 15 important events or milestones that shaped your life. These events should be good and bad experiences and represent events or milestones that shaped who you are today.

- For each event or milestone, write your age (or approximate age), the year, who you were (in personality) before and after the event/milestone, and key persons such as a mentor, bad influence, or symbol that played a role in the event/milestone (if applicable), the setting, and location of the event/milestone.

EXPECTED RESULTS

- A list of 10 to 15 life events or milestones arranged in chronological order.

- A collection of foundational experiences that you can draw upon to create your story's outline.

- A clearer understanding of the journey you'll be sharing, highlighting the events that shaped your story of resilience, growth, and victory.

"Every milestone is a chapter in the story of who you are. Together, they create the path that leads to your greatest truth."

DAY 5

GOAL: Identify Key Themes

Today, you'll be exploring the central themes of your list of events and milestones. Thus, you will need to refer to the list that you generated yesterday.

Themes are the underlying ideas or messages that weave through your experiences, giving your memoir depth and meaning. Think about the big lessons or recurring topics in your life—perhaps resilience, faith, relationship issues, or personal growth. Identifying these themes will help bring cohesion to your story and ensure that readers understand the core message you want to share.

In a quiet space, take a moment to reflect on the themes that feel most relevant to your journey. Consider the lessons you've learned, the patterns you've noticed, or the values you hold close. Then, look at your list of events and milestones. Do you see a pattern? Do you see a theme connecting each event (good or bad)? Do you see a climax or a shift take place? These elements are key to ensuring that each event/milestone has a theme that connects to the bigger theme and goal of the overall book.

After this activity, work through the prompts to start pinpointing and writing the key themes that will guide each event/milestone of your memoir. Write your responses, listing two or three main themes that feel authentic and significant to your story.

TIME COMMITMENT

45 minutes to 60 minutes

PROMPTS

- For each event/milestone, write at least three themes that you see occurring from the events/milestone.

- Write at least one sentence to capture the message of each event/milestone.

- After completing the first two prompts, what recurring topics, issues, themes, or circumstances do you see? Write them down as a separate list. Note: Often, these recurring items connect event to event as you go in order from one event/milestone to the next.

- Is there a climax or turning point in your list of events and milestones? If so, take special note of this, as it will be the turning point of your manuscript.

EXPECTED RESULTS

- A list of two to three central themes that will anchor your story.

- A foundation of themes that gives structure and focus to each chapter of your memoir.

- Increased clarity about the big-picture ideas you hope to convey.

"Your themes are the heartbeat of your story; let them shape your words and guide readers toward the wisdom of your journey."

DAY 6

GOAL: The Thread

We all know that a thread has a starting point and an endpoint, weaving everything together along its path. Your life story is no different—it's a thread, a journey that begins with your earliest experiences and leads to the place where you now stand as the victor, the healed, or the transformed individual ready to share your truth. That thread is what ties your story together, and today, your goal is to identify it.

Reflect on the activities you completed for Days 5 and 6. The thread you're looking for is the main idea of your book—the central message you want to share with your audience or the one specific person you're writing to. This overarching theme should naturally emerge from the events, milestones, and lessons you've already mapped out.

Before diving into the prompts, take a moment to revisit your timeline of events and milestones, the themes you identified, and the significant turning points in your life. Look at how everything—both the good and the bad—intertwines to create your story. Observe the connections and patterns that arise. This is not the time to force a particular theme into your story but to let the raw information you've captured guide you.

Allow your reflections to reveal the main idea or message that ties your story together. Let your journey speak for itself, showing you the thread that runs through it all, shaping the heart of your book.

TIME COMMITMENT

30 minutes to 60 minutes

PROMPTS

- Look back at your timeline of events and milestones. What patterns or recurring themes stand out to you?

- What is the common lesson or transformation these events seem to point toward?

- If you had to summarize the message of your story in one sentence, what would it be?

- How do your experiences, both good and bad, connect to this overarching theme?

- When you reflect on where you are today, what truth or insight has guided your journey?

EXPECTED RESULTS

- A clear understanding of the main idea or theme that threads through your life story.

- A one-sentence summary of the core message of your book.

- A deeper connection to your story's purpose and its impact on your intended audience.

"Your life is a tapestry of moments, woven together by a thread of resilience, transformation, and truth. Find your thread—it's the key to your story."

DAY 7

GOAL: Write Your Outline

Now that you've identified the main theme of your book, it's time to lock it in. Remember, this theme isn't something you impose upon your story—it emerges naturally from the events, milestones, and reflections of your life. For some of you, this process may have revealed a deeper, more profound message than you initially expected. That's a beautiful discovery because it means you now have a clearer understanding of your life's true story and purpose.

With your theme in place, the next step is to create your chapter outline. Reflect on the work you completed in the previous days, and begin crafting chapter titles for each event or milestone you wrote down. Ideally, you should have 10 to 15 events, though some may need to be combined into a single chapter. For example, if Event 3 and Event 4 are closely connected, they could form Chapter 3. This way, your outline will naturally flow and reflect the thread of your story.

Your outline is the backbone of your memoir. It ties each chapter together, creating a cohesive journey toward your book's central message. As you develop your chapter titles, don't be overly critical. Whatever comes to mind first is often the best choice. Keep titles concise yet intriguing—phrases that spark curiosity or reflect the core lesson of the chapter. Titles can take the form of statements, questions, or even impactful quotes from those moments in your life. Let them invite readers into your story.

TIME COMMITMENT

30 minutes to 60 minutes

PROMPTS

- Revisit your timeline and list of events and milestones. Which ones stand alone as chapters, and which ones naturally connect to form a single chapter?

- For each chapter, write a title that captures the essence of the event or milestone.

  - Example: For an event where you overcame a significant challenge, your title could be "The Day Everything Changed" or "From Struggle to Strength."

- How do the chapter titles flow together to create the thread of your story? Does the progression reflect your journey toward the main theme?

- Are your chapter titles intriguing and inviting? Do they inspire curiosity or hint at the deeper lessons in your story?

Note: Don't be afraid of writing a few chapter title ideas and then picking the one that resonates the most with the content you will write about.

EXPECTED RESULTS

- A clear and organized chapter outline that reflects the main theme of your book.

- Chapter titles that are concise, intriguing, and connected to your life's key events and milestones.

- A roadmap for your memoir that will guide you through the writing phase.

"Your chapters are the stepping stones of your story, each title a window into the moments that shaped your journey. Let them invite readers into the heart of your truth."

Writing Days (Days 8–23)

Guidelines for Writing Days

Writing Days are when your vision becomes a reality. Each day is dedicated to creating a complete draft of one chapter of your memoir, covering the key events, milestones, and themes identified in your outline. You'll aim to write a full chapter daily, focusing on reaching around **2,000 to 2,500 words**. If you happen to go over, that's fine; the goal is to hit this word count consistently, ensuring that each chapter feels complete and offers your readers a balanced depth of insight.

This is the part of the process you've been waiting for—the writing itself. Days 8-23 are the culmination of your hard work and planning. These are the days when the words you've been holding inside will come to life on the page. For so long, you've wrestled with the idea of writing your story, held back by doubts or overwhelmed by the size of it all. But now, you're ready. You've been dreaming about writing this book for years, and now you're equipped with a structured plan to guide you to completion.

This moment might bring you some excitement and feelings of apprehension. You might feel fear, hesitation, self-doubt, or a combination. And that's perfectly okay. This is your story, and it's a story worth telling. If you need to, embrace the phrase of **"Do It Scared."** Think of other times when you went into something new without knowing how it would turn out. You might have stumbled the first time you spoke in front of people; the first time you drove, you probably felt nervous. Yet you pushed forward, learned, and grew through each experience. The same goes for writing your memoir—it's a new chapter of growth, even if you have to take it on with a bit of fear.

Using the Daily Articles

The daily articles may not always align with the specific phase of writing you're in at the moment. Like I said, the goals of Days 8 to 23 are geared towards you writing a chapter each day. However, each day, I share an article with you that tackles a different aspect of the writing journey to encourage and keep you going. These articles reflect the experiences of many aspiring authors I've coached, addressing the highs and lows they encounter. Use them as a toolkit: don't hesitate to re-read articles on days when you need extra support, encouragement, or guidance. Think of these articles as companions through your writing journey—always there to lend advice or reassurance as you move from one chapter to the next.

Daily Structure and Focus

Each Writing Day begins with you reading the daily article or "lesson." Then, it's time to write your chapter for that day.

Your *Time Commitment* for all writing days (unless otherwise noted) should be at least 2 hours. Some days, you will use all of this time and may even desire to add more. As you continue with Writing Days, you may begin to become more proficient during these days. However, try not to skimp on the time commitment on Writing Days.

For the event(s) or milestone(s), you're writing into the chapter, also reflect on the message(s), themes, and lessons learned.

Further, review the notes that you generated during days 1 to 7. Use those notes to spark your thoughts and progress toward your 2,000-word count.

To help you progress through the chapter, your chapter for each day will follow a simple structure:

- **Opening Paragraph(s):** Introduce the focus of the chapter and set the stage for the events to unfold.

- **Body of the Chapter:** Dive into the key events, memories, and experiences connected to the chapter's theme. Describe what happened, who was involved, and how these experiences shaped you. Remember to reflect on how you felt before and after each event and explore the lessons learned.

- **Sub-Sections:** Don't be afraid to have sub-sections of the chapter. For example, if the Chapter title is: My Earliest Memory of Mom," there might be a culmination of several themes or accounts I want to share. Thus, I can have the chapter title and then have sub-sections with their titles, including "My Mother is Beautiful," "At 5 Years Old," and "Cooking with Mom at Age 7." While the chapter is geared towards 'my one early memory of mom,' I share multiple memories to build the full memory of mom. You can use sub-sections as well.

- **Closing Paragraph(s):** Wrap up with a conclusion that ties back to the theme, reflects on what the chapter reveals about you, and perhaps hints at what's to come.

Remember

This time is about creating, not perfecting. It's about writing your first manuscript draft. Focus on getting your story written in raw form that is as authentic and full as possible. So, don't worry about perfection; focus on expression. Let go of the need to be flawless. Let your story emerge raw and real, knowing that the time for editing and refining will come later.

On your writing journey, you're one step ahead with an outline, a purpose, and a plan. Now, your only task is to write. Take it one day at a time, one chapter at a time. The rest will fall into place.

DAY 8

GOAL: FINDING DIRECTION IN YOUR STORY

Writing can sometimes leave us feeling uncertain about where to start or how to capture an experience with the detail and emotion it deserves. This isn't writer's block or an emotional block—it's more of a need for clarity on bringing an event to life on the page. When you find yourself in this space, guiding questions can be powerful tools to help you break down the moment and build it into a vivid, meaningful part of your story. Here are some questions to help you dive deeper when you're feeling stuck.

1. What happened before, during, and after this event?

Start by thinking of the broader context. What events led up to this experience? By establishing what happened before, during, and after, you create a natural flow for the narrative and allow readers to understand the event's significance within the larger story. Describing the sequence around an event also helps ground you in the moment, making it easier to write with authenticity.

2. What were my thoughts and feelings at the time?

Reflecting on your emotions and mindset during the event brings depth to your writing. Ask yourself, "What was I thinking? How did I feel?" These details are often the most relatable to readers. By expressing both the internal dialogue and emotions you experienced, you invite readers to connect with your journey on a personal level.

3. How did this event change my perspective or direction?

Consider how this experience shaped or shifted your path. Did it alter the way you viewed yourself, others, or the world? Did it impact your goals or values? Reflecting on these changes shows

29

your growth, adding layers to your story and helping readers see your development.

4. What was my biggest takeaway or lesson learned?

Every impactful event holds a lesson or insight. Identify the main takeaway from the experience. What did you learn, and how did that lesson stick with you? Sharing these insights not only enriches your memoir but also helps readers find value and meaning in your story.

5. Who or what influenced the outcome, and how?

Reflect on the people, circumstances, or elements that played a role in shaping this event's outcome. Was there a mentor, a friend, or even an unexpected twist that guided the direction? Acknowledging these influences helps provide a fuller picture of the experience and allows readers to see the interconnectedness of people and events in your life.

I find that asking yourself these questions when you seek direction in writing your manuscript allows you to flow and create a wealth of content for your book. At the same time, after writing and answering these questions, you're able to read the account and decide what's required to capture the heart of the content. Therefore, removing unnecessary context or thoughts. Sometimes writing the full account helps you reach the heart of the approach to sharing the lessons learned.

Use these guiding questions whenever you feel stuck, and allow them to prompt new layers of detail and meaning in your writing. They can help bring clarity to your story, transforming a complex experience into a clear, compelling part of your memoir.

DAY 9

GOAL: BREAKING THROUGH WRITER'S BLOCK

Writer's block is a natural part of the writing process. Almost every writer has faced the challenge of staring at a blank page, feeling that the words are just out of reach. When this happens, take a deep breath and remember there are ways to get "unstuck" and back into the flow. Here are five effective strategies to help you regain your momentum.

1. Try Free-Writing

Free-writing can release your mind from the constraints of writer's block. Set a timer for five or ten minutes and write without stopping or censoring yourself. Forget about grammar, spelling, or structure—just let your thoughts spill onto the page. This exercise can help clear mental clutter and spark unexpected insights, often providing the inspiration needed to continue your story.

2. Step Away for a Short Break

Sometimes, the best way to move forward is by stepping back. When writer's block starts to overwhelm you, give yourself permission to take a short break—stretch, walk, or take a few deep breaths. Shift your focus away from writing and onto the present moment. When you return, you'll often find that your mind feels clearer and ready to write.

3. Change Your Scenery

A simple change of environment can reignite creativity. If you've been writing in the same spot, try moving to a new location, like a coffee shop, park, or a different room. Changing scenery can stimulate your senses and give you a fresh perspective on your story.

4. Revisit an Inspiring Book or Quote

When words don't come, turn to the words of others. Re-read a favorite book, poem, or motivational quote. Reconnecting with inspiring words can remind you of the power of storytelling and often provides just the spark you need to return to your own writing.

5. Break Down Your Chapter into Smaller Parts

Writer's block can sometimes come from feeling overwhelmed by the size of the task. Instead of tackling a whole chapter, focus on one small section, like an event or conversation. Completing a smaller portion of your story can build momentum and make the process more manageable.

Remember, writer's block is just a temporary pause. I've dealt with it several times during multiple books, and it's normal to experience it. I've used and shared the examples written here with others and you should use them in your writing journey.

Approach writer's block patiently, take breaks when needed, and trust that the words will return to you in time.

DAY 10

GOAL: BREAKING THROUGH EMOTIONAL BLOCKS

When it comes to writing our deepest experiences, we often encounter emotional blocks, especially when revisiting sensitive or painful memories. These moments from the past can feel heavy, and facing them on the page might seem overwhelming. But approaching these memories with gentleness and compassion can transform them from burdens into powerful stories that resonate with truth. Here are some techniques to help you break through emotional blocks and let your story flow.

1. Embrace Vulnerability

Begin by acknowledging the emotions connected to your memories. Let yourself feel the vulnerability that arises; it's part of the journey and can deepen your writing. Don't pressure yourself to share every detail or fully relive the experience. Instead, write as if you're offering a glimpse into the heart of what you went through. This approach gives you control over how much to reveal and helps make the writing process feel safer and more manageable.

2. Focus on the Lessons Learned

Rather than solely revisiting the pain, focus on what each experience taught you. What insights did you gain? How did these moments shape who you are? By concentrating on the lessons rather than just the hardships, you'll find that your writing takes on a tone of resilience and growth. This focus allows you to write about tough times with a perspective that uplifts both you and your readers.

3. Use Sensory Details to Ground the Experience

Describe the environment, the sounds, the sights, or even the smells. These details allow you to bring readers into the scene while creating distance from the emotional intensity. Sensory descriptions keep you grounded in the narrative, allowing you to relay what happened with clarity.

4. Write with Compassion for Yourself

When revisiting painful memories, remind yourself to be gentle. Don't rush the process or judge your feelings; simply let them surface as you write. Allow space for self-compassion as you bring these moments to life, acknowledging the strength it took to survive and grow beyond them.

5. Give Yourself Permission to Pause

Writing about emotional experiences can be taxing, and sometimes, a pause is necessary. Give yourself permission to take breaks, step back, and come back when you feel ready. A story written with compassion—both for yourself and your experiences—is one that resonates with authenticity.

6. It's Your First Draft

Not knowing if what you write is too much information is not of concern at this point. The key is to write what you want. Once it's written, you can read what you wrote and decide if you need to add or remove some information. Further, once your editor is involved, they will help you work through and decide what information is relevant. Lastly, it's your manuscript. If, after edits, you're not comfortable, remove it all together. But for your first draft, write it all.

Approaching emotional memories with kindness creates a safe space for healing, allowing you to share your story in a way that honors your journey and connects deeply with your readers.

DAY 11

GOAL: FOCUS ON CONTENT, NOT PERFECTION

When starting your first draft, it's easy to feel the urge to make every sentence shine. You want your words to flow perfectly, your grammar to be flawless, and every thought to read like poetry. But the truth is, a first draft is simply that—the beginning. Its job isn't to be perfect; it's to capture your ideas, thoughts, and memories to lay the groundwork for your story. So, the key with your first draft is to write what's in your head and get it down on paper (onto your laptop).

I recall that before working on the book titled *The Art of Finishing*, I had all the book's content in my head. I wouldn't set aside the time to write. But one day, the inspiration and time hit me at the same time, and I began to write. I didn't care about the spelling or the grammar. I kept typing and typing. I thought of that experience as if it was a 'brain dump' or 'brain purge' where I just had the urge to get everything in my head onto the pages, and this type of action is what's key for you right now. Don't be perfect. Just write.

Here's why focusing on content over perfection is important.

1. Embrace the Messiness of the First Draft

The first draft is your creative playground, where you explore ideas without the pressure of perfection. Let your words spill onto the page in their raw form. Don't worry about grammar, spelling, or elegant sentences right now; these can all be polished later. Allow yourself to be messy because within that mess lies the true heart of your story.

2. Trust the Process: Content Comes First

Writing is a process, and perfectionism can slow you down. Right now, your goal is to get your story out of your mind and onto the page. Each time you sit down to write, think of yourself as simply capturing the essence of your story. The words may not be perfect, but they are real. Focus on conveying the core of your ideas, and trust that you'll have time to refine them later.

3. Silence Your Inner Critic

That little voice telling you every sentence needs to be "just right" before moving on? Gently ignore it. The inner critic has its place in the editing phase, but it can stifle creativity during drafting. Remind yourself that there will be time for revision, but today's job is to express, not perfect.

4. Reframe Mistakes as Part of the Journey

Grammar, spelling, and style can all be improved, but the ideas and authenticity of your first draft are priceless. Embrace any imperfections as part of the journey, knowing that each sentence, even if rough, brings you closer to a complete story.

5. Remember: Writing is Rewriting

A first draft is simply the beginning. Writing is rewriting—each revision will bring you closer to the polished piece you envision. For now, let your thoughts flow freely. You'll find clarity and focus as you revisit and refine in later drafts.

By letting go of the need for perfection, you allow yourself to truly write, capturing your story's raw and honest foundation. So breathe, trust yourself, and enjoy the journey of your first draft.

DAY 12

GOAL: WRITING WITH INTEGRITY

When writing a memoir, it's easy to feel the temptation to embellish. Sometimes, we wonder if our experiences are "interesting enough" or if readers will find our stories engaging. But remember, your story is powerful, just as it is. Staying true to the facts and the authenticity of your experiences allows readers to connect with you on a real, meaningful level. Here are some tips to help you stay grounded in your truth and write with integrity.

1. Let the Impact Speak for Itself

Every experience you've included in your memoir has impacted you deeply. Rather than dressing up the details, focus on how each event shaped you. What was the lesson learned? How did it change your perspective? By emphasizing the significance of the moment, you allow its true power to shine through without adding unnecessary embellishments. This approach not only respects your journey but also keeps your writing raw and real.

2. Trust Your Story

It's easy to fall into the trap of thinking your story needs more "drama" to hold a reader's attention. Trust that the realness of your story is what makes it compelling. Readers are drawn to genuine voices and authentic experiences. Trusting your story allows you to let go of the urge to overemphasize details, enabling you to stay grounded in the honesty of your journey.

3. Embrace the Ordinary Moments

Some of the most powerful parts of a story come from ordinary, everyday moments. These are the spaces where readers see themselves in your life and where your journey resonates most deeply. Don't feel pressured to skip or enhance these moments; instead, embrace them as part of your narrative. The beauty of a memoir often lies in these relatable experiences.

4. Avoid Comparison

As you write, it can be tempting to compare your story to those of others, especially if you've read memoirs with dramatic twists and turns. Remember that your story is unique, but your truths reach many. Let go of any pressure to make it fit someone else's style or level of excitement. Focus on telling *your* story, knowing that its authenticity is what will make it memorable.

5. Keep the Focus on Your Emotions and Growth

One of the best ways to tell your story honestly is by focusing on your own emotional journey. Highlight your thoughts, feelings, and growth through each event, rather than getting caught up in extra details. This approach allows readers to connect with the human side of your story and keeps your narrative deeply personal.

When you stick to the facts and stay true to yourself, your story gains power. Readers will feel the integrity of your words and connect with the sincerity of your journey. By focusing on the impact, growth, and realness of your experiences, you allow the authenticity of your story to resonate fully—just as it's meant to be told.

DAY 13

GOAL: USING CONVERSATIONS

Sometimes, the best way to clarify our ideas isn't through solitary reflection but by engaging in conversation. Talking with family members, friends, or even mentors can provide fresh perspectives that help shape and refine our stories. The right conversation can shine a light on areas we may have overlooked, helping us connect the dots and see our ideas more clearly. Here's how reaching out to others can help you unlock new depths in your writing.

1. Choose Someone Who Understands Your Vision

Select a person who genuinely understands your goals and respects the purpose behind your memoir. This could be a friend who knows your story well, a family member with insight into your experiences, or even a mentor with a tact for asking the right questions. Their connection to your journey makes them more likely to offer feedback that's both thoughtful and relevant to the message you want to convey.

2. Let Them Ask Questions

Sometimes, the simple act of answering questions can bring unexpected clarity. Allow your conversation partner to ask about the themes, events, or characters in your account. Questions like "What was the turning point in that experience?" or "How did this event change you?" can open up new insights. By explaining things out loud, you may find yourself discovering connections or themes that were previously unclear.

3. Discussing Different Angles

Engaging in conversation allows you to explore different angles you might not have considered. A friend or mentor might suggest a perspective you hadn't thought of, which can enhance the depth of your writing. Talking through these viewpoints can enrich your story and provide valuable input on how to approach complex themes or events.

4. Use the Conversation to Strengthen Your Focus

Sometimes, writing can veer off track, or certain details can feel murky. A good conversation can help refocus your ideas, enabling you to clarify your main themes or fine-tune your chapter structure. Talking things out can also help you determine which details to strengthen and which to remove to keep your story compelling and cohesive.

5. Capture Insights as Soon as Possible

After a conversation, jot down any key insights or fresh ideas while they're still fresh. These notes will serve as guideposts when you return to writing, helping you remember the inspiration and direction gained from your discussion.

A major attribute of my one-on-one sessions with aspiring authors is ensuring that they are inspired and have clarity. These conversations are often highlighted by the aspiring author, saying, "I feel the weight lifted off of me." Finding a connection to a deeper meaning of life's experiences always leads to inspired and clear thoughts and words.

A thoughtful conversation can bring much-needed clarity to your writing process, adding a perspective that might not have emerged otherwise. Embrace the guidance, the questions, and the new ideas that a trusted person can offer—they may hold the key to refining your story in ways you never anticipated.

DAY 14

GOAL: PROTECTING PRIVACY

Writing a memoir means revisiting real experiences, often involving people who played significant roles in your story. But telling your truth doesn't mean compromising others' privacy. Hitting the right balance allows you to share openly while protecting the identities of those involved. Here are a few ways to approach this delicate area of writing.

1. Decide When to Use Real Names

Sometimes, using real names is necessary to tell your story authentically—especially when discussing family members or close friends who have agreed to be part of your narrative. However, it's essential to be mindful and consider if including real names truly adds value. When in doubt, remember that using a name should serve your story and not distract from it.

2. Use Pseudonyms for Clarity

When real names aren't essential, fictionalized names can offer clarity and privacy. Changing a name doesn't change the essence of what happened, and it allows you to share details without exposing someone's identity. Consider pseudonyms, particularly for sensitive topics or when addressing people who may prefer not to be mentioned directly. You can also include a note at the beginning of your book explaining that some names have been changed to respect privacy.

3. Refer to Roles, Not Names

Sometimes, the best way to protect privacy is to refer to someone by their role rather than their name. For instance, rather than mentioning "Jane" or "Uncle John," you could say "a close friend" or "a family member." This method focuses on the significance of their role in your story rather than their specific identity, maintaining respect for their privacy while ensuring your narrative remains impactful.

4. Frame the Event, Not the Person

When describing sensitive moments, center your writing on the event and its impact on you, rather than on the individual involved. Focus on the lesson, emotions, or growth that came from the experience, allowing readers to connect with your journey. This approach helps keep the story personal and reflective, without putting unnecessary attention on others' actions.

5. Keep the Focus on Your Story

Ultimately, a memoir is about *your* experiences and insights. When you stay true to *your* perspective, it becomes easier to tell *your* story without feeling the need to reveal everything about everyone involved. This balance allows you to share honestly while respecting others' privacy.

Your first draft is still your first draft. So, don't be afraid to share your truths. In the good experiences, using a person's name may not impact their privacy, but in those bad experiences, when things take you into a dark place, consider your approach. But don't stop writing.

Writing with this balance of openness and respect not only strengthens your story but honors the people in your life. It allows you to express your truth authentically, ensuring that both you and your readers gain the insights your journey has to offer.

DAY 15

GOAL: BUILDING CONTEXT AND CLARITY

You've been writing for a few days now, and today's article is a topic you need to consider as you move forward.

When writing your memoir, it's easy to assume that readers will intuitively understand the emotions, settings, and significance of your manuscript's moments. However, one of the most effective ways to truly connect with your readers is to write as if no one knows what you've been through or fully grasps your unique perspective. Imagine you're the only one who has walked this path and that you need to provide every detail to bring your readers along with you. Don't get me wrong; you're already writing specifically for the person who is your audience. At the same time, it's important to ensure that you share the context with clarity so even that person knows what you mean and does not assume what you meant.

1. Assume Nothing

Think of your readers as if they're from a completely different world, unfamiliar with the emotions, people, and places that shaped your experiences. Just as a mathematician wouldn't assume that everyone understands complex equations, don't assume that readers automatically know what you mean when you refer to pivotal events or feelings. Approach your story as if no one has context, and give them the necessary background to fully appreciate each part of your journey.

2. Build the Scene with Details

When recounting an experience, set the stage for your readers. Describe the environment, the time of day, the atmosphere, and any physical details that bring the moment to life. Help readers visualize where you were, what was happening around you, and the sensory experiences that grounded you in that place. This approach not only makes your story richer but also creates a clear picture that readers can follow, even if they have no firsthand knowledge of what you've been through.

3. Convey the Emotions

The emotional landscape of your story is just as important as the physical setting. Don't shy away from expressing the full range of feelings you experienced, whether it was fear, excitement, heartbreak, or joy. Describe not only how you felt but also why those emotions were significant. By doing this, you make it easier for readers to empathize and connect with your experience on a personal level, even if they've never been in a similar situation.

4. Explain the Meaning and Impact

For each event you recount, explain its importance. Why does it matter to your story? How did it shape you? Assume that readers are hearing it for the first time and need insight into why this moment stands out in your life. Providing this level of explanation ensures that your message comes across clearly, helping readers understand not just what happened but why it mattered.

5. Let Your Voice Be Your Guide

Finally, write with your authentic voice. Write to that one person as if they're sitting in front of you, and you're speaking directly to them. Don't let them guess what you mean; instead, take the time to explain, paint a vivid picture, and convey your perspective fully.

Writing as if no one knows what you've been through ensures that your story is accessible, relatable, and rich with context, allowing your readers to walk alongside you and experience your journey as vividly as you did.

DAY 16

GOAL: HANDLING SUDDEN INSPIRATION

Writing brings its rhythm, but inspiration can be unpredictable. Sometimes, in the midst of a routine, a new idea or memory strikes with clarity, adding richness to your story. These moments of sudden inspiration are valuable, but it's important to capture them without losing focus on your current work. Here are some practical ways to capture inspiration on-the-go and ensure it supports your writing journey.

1. Use Voice Notes to Capture Thoughts Instantly

If you're out and about—perhaps on a train or in the car—jotting down a new idea can be challenging. In these moments, use the voice notes feature on your phone to record your thoughts. This way, you're able to capture the essence of your inspiration without needing to write it out immediately. Listening back to these recordings later can be like accessing a spark of creativity that you might have otherwise forgotten.

2. Take Advantage of Dictation Features

Most smartphones and electronic software, including Microsoft Word and Google Documents, have a dictation feature that allows you to speak your ideas, which are then transcribed into text. I use this feature ALL THE TIME. I even used it as I developed this book.

Whether you're walking, commuting, or simply unable to type, dictation can be a helpful way to capture new ideas in real-time.

3. Keep a Notebook or Note App Ready

If you prefer writing things down, carry a small notebook or use a notes app on your phone. Jot down any thoughts, phrases, or descriptions that come to mind, knowing that you can expand on them later. By storing these flashes of insight in one place, you'll be able to revisit them when you're ready to develop them fully, without losing track of where they fit in your story.

4. Pause to Reflect—Then Return to Your Current Task

Sometimes, inspiration can feel urgent, pulling your focus from your current chapter. When this happens, take a moment to acknowledge the new idea. Write a quick summary or voice note.

I've had to use this tip at several points during writing. I could be writing one particular part of the manuscript, and suddenly inspiration hits, but for another chapter. I quickly started writing what I was inspired to write. Once it was over, I then returned to what I was working on.

This approach allows you to honor the inspiration without letting it derail your current writing task.

5. Schedule Time to Revisit Your Ideas

Set aside time each week to review any notes, voice recordings, or quick ideas that struck you throughout your writing days. This practice gives you an organized way to incorporate new thoughts without interrupting your daily writing flow, keeping both your inspiration and your focused momentum intact.

Embrace these moments of inspiration as valuable additions to your memoir, but stay grounded in your writing process. Capturing your thoughts as they come will ensure they're ready for when you need them, allowing you to incorporate fresh ideas seamlessly. Let each burst of inspiration enrich your story, adding depth and authenticity to the chapters you create.

DAY 17

On Day 3, I had you "Define Your Audience." since you've been writing chapter after chapter for several days now, I thought it necessary to ensure that the one person you've identified as your ideal reader is in focus. This single individual embodies the heart of your audience and serves as your anchor when the writing process feels overwhelming. Writing as if you're speaking directly to that one person ensures that your story remains authentic, purposeful, and deeply impactful.

1. Speak Directly to Their Struggles

Your reader isn't looking for perfection; they're looking for connection. Think about the challenges they've faced—the moments of doubt, fear, or triumph. Write as if you're sitting across from them, sharing your story in a way that helps them see themselves in your journey. Your words are not just for you; they are a lifeline for someone seeking clarity, comfort, or inspiration.

2. Make It Personal and Relatable

When you write for one, you tap into the intimacy of conversation. Use language that feels natural, as if you're confiding in a friend. Avoid overly complex ideas or unnecessary details that might distract from your core message. The goal is to create a sense of understanding, where your reader feels seen and heard through your words.

3. Focus on Emotional Resonance

Your one reader connects to your story through emotion. Write with honesty and vulnerability, allowing your feelings to guide your narrative. Whether you're sharing joy, pain, or growth, let the emotional core of your story speak directly to their heart. The authenticity of your emotions will ripple through every page, drawing your reader in and leaving a lasting impression.

4. Stay Aligned With Your Purpose

Remember why you started writing this book. Your purpose is to help, inspire, or educate someone through your story. By keeping your ideal reader in mind, you ensure that every sentence you write aligns with that purpose. This clarity not only strengthens your narrative but also keeps you motivated to finish what you've started.

5. Trust the Ripple Effect

Though you're writing to one, the impact of your words will extend far beyond them. Your ideal reader represents the countless others who will see themselves in your story. Trust that by focusing on this single individual, your book will find its way to all the people who need it most.

There are over 7 billion people in this world. It may seem foolish to write to one person, but your writing will never be scattered when you write to them. You will never be talking about two events at the same time. Rather, you will stay on track and in your lane. Further, that one person you're writing to actually has a line of people behind them who need to read your book. So, the focus you have in writing to one will ensure that you reach millions.

DAY 18

GOAL: USING DIALOGUE EFFECTIVELY

In memoir writing, dialogue can be one of the most powerful tools to draw readers into your world. It's not just about recounting what was said; it's about recreating the setting, mood, and connection these conversations hold. Using dialogue strategically allows readers to feel like they're right there with you, witnessing the exchanges that shaped your journey.

1. When to Use Dialogue

Dialogue works best when you want to highlight an important interaction or milestone. Conversations that reveal insights, evoke strong emotions or change the course of your story deserve attention.

- **A heartfelt conversation with a parent** that changed your perspective.

- **A challenging talk with a friend** that tested your values or boundaries.

- **An inspiring exchange with a mentor or teacher** who influenced your goals.

- **A memorable interaction with a stranger** that left a lasting impression.

- **A conversation with a role model or public figure** that motivated you to take action.

Bringing these exchanges to life with dialogue can add layers of meaning and authenticity.

2. Show Character Through Conversation

Dialogue is a great way to reveal character traits—both yours and those of the people in your story. For example, if you include a conversation with your father, you might capture the way he always spoke with a steady, reassuring tone, even during tough discussions. If you include a humorous exchange with a friend, it can highlight the bond you share. Letting these traits come through in the way people speak and interact helps readers understand them as real, relatable figures in your life.

4. How to Write Dialogue

Writing dialogue isn't hard but does require that you pay attention. You have to play tennis with the dialogue. One person says something, and then the other says something. You must keep that going back and forth while adding character to that conversation. Don't get carried away with all the punctuation marks required in written dialogue. Although they play a critical role in the published version of your book, as you write your first draft, it's important to get the content.

5. Use Internal Dialogue to Show Personal Growth

Internal dialogue—your thoughts and reflections—can be equally powerful, especially during pivotal moments. Whether grappling with self-doubt, finding courage, or processing a loss, sharing your inner thoughts allows readers to connect with your personal journey.

Incorporating dialogue in your memoir enriches your story, making it more engaging and relatable. These moments of exchange give readers insight into your relationships, thoughts, and growth, making them feel like they're right there with you, witnessing every word.

DAY 19

Writing is an active process, but it doesn't always mean using your fingers on the keyboard or pen to paper for every moment of your writing session. Sometimes, progress means pausing, reflecting, and reconnecting with your purpose. The 60-120 minutes you've committed to your daily writing sessions aren't solely about producing words; they're about building the story, clarifying your thoughts, and ensuring that your work stays aligned with your goals.

Here are activities that you will naturally participate in during your writing sessions.

1. Use Reflection to Stay on Track

Sometimes, you will need to take a moment to review what you've already written. Rereading previous chapters or sections helps you reconnect with your story's tone, themes, and flow. It's like stretching before exercise—it prepares your mind to work effectively and ensures you remain consistent with your narrative. When you reread, it's not the time to edit, but to reflect and connect with what you left off writing and begin to continue writing.

2. Revisit Your Pre-Writing Work

Your outline, notes, and prompts from the first seven days are valuable tools. If you're feeling stuck or unsure how to continue, revisit these resources. They will remind you of your book's overarching theme and provide clarity on how each chapter ties into the bigger picture. Trust your preparation—it was designed to guide you during moments like this.

3. Create a Roadmap for a Chapter

Sometimes, writing a chapter requires more than the outline you prepared during the first 7-Days. If a chapter feels particularly complex, take a few minutes to sketch a roadmap for it. Identify how one idea connects to the next and how these connections align with the lessons, themes, or events you're sharing. Having a chapter outline will help you keep momentum when writing.

4. Read for Inspiration

On days when the words aren't flowing, reread articles from this 30-Day plan that resonate with your current challenge. Whether it's overcoming writer's block or emotional barriers, revisiting these insights can reignite your passion and help you refocus your efforts.

5. Don't Fear the Pause

Pausing during a writing session doesn't mean failure. In fact, taking a moment to breathe, reflect, or recalibrate your thoughts is often necessary for quality writing. These pauses allow you to step back, view your work from a fresh perspective, and ensure that every sentence serves your purpose.

Writing isn't about rushing to fill the page; it's about creating a manuscript worth reading. By the end of each writing session, you want to feel like the time spent was well spent. You want to feel accomplished and feel like you progressed.

DAY 20

GOAL: WRITING AND TRAVELING

For many of us, the ideal writing environment is a familiar, quiet space that allows us to focus fully on our words. But life doesn't always accommodate our routines, and sometimes, we find ourselves needing to write in new places or while traveling.

Whether you're away for work, on vacation, or simply out of your regular space, it's possible to maintain your momentum. Here are some practical tips to help you adapt your writing process, no matter where you are.

1. Create a Portable Writing Kit

Put together a small, dedicated writing kit that you can easily take with you. Include essentials like your laptop or notebook, pens, headphones, and any reference materials you might need. Having a ready-to-go kit will help you set up quickly and bring a touch of familiarity wherever you are. This small collection of tools can be a powerful anchor, signaling to your mind that it's time to focus on writing.

2. Find a Quiet or Comfortable Spot

When writing on the go, look for a space that feels comfortable and as distraction-free as possible. It could be a quiet corner in a café, a park bench, or a space with minimal foot traffic. Even if it's not your usual setup, find a place where you feel relatively relaxed and undisturbed. This small act of choosing your environment mindfully can help ease your transition and keep you centered.

3. Use Headphones to Create Your Own Space

Sometimes, new environments come with unexpected sounds. Listening to calming music or ambient sounds can create a mental "bubble," helping you stay focused and block out distractions. Headphones also serve as a signal to people around you that you're engaged in something important, reducing the chance of interruptions.

4. Set Short Writing Sessions

When in a new space, it can be challenging to stay focused for long stretches. Break your writing into shorter sessions, such as 20- or 30-minute blocks, followed by a brief break. This approach keeps you productive without overwhelming yourself and can help you stay in a writing rhythm despite the unfamiliar surroundings.

5. Embrace Flexibility

Sometimes, the writing process in a new place might feel a bit different than usual, and that's okay. Embrace the spontaneity and adjust your expectations. If you don't achieve your usual word count, focus on capturing meaningful ideas instead. Writing in a new space can often inspire unexpected insights, adding fresh perspectives to your work.

Whenever I travel, I still continue to write, and you can do it too. Even if, during this 30-day challenge, you find the need to travel for whatever reason, stay committed to the process.

Adapting your writing process while traveling or in new spaces takes a bit of patience and flexibility. With a portable setup, mindful choice of environment, and a focus on the essentials, you can keep your momentum going no matter where you are. Embrace the change of scenery as an opportunity to see your story from a new angle.

DAY 21

GOAL: CRAFTING YOUR BOOK TITLE

The Book Title is everything! It's the main phrase that attracts people to a book. It's probably something that attracted you to *this* book. Thus, the goal of this article is to help you create a compelling, reader-centered book title with an impactful subtheme that resonates with your intended audience, drawing them in with a clear sense of the book's purpose and appeal.

CONCEPTS TO HELP CRAFT YOUR TITLE:

1. **Separate Yourself from the Title You Had in Mind**

   You may already have a working title, but try to let go of it. Sometimes, the titles we initially come up with are based solely on our own interpretations. Your readers may not have the same context, so creating a fresh title ensures that you're choosing words that resonate with them, not just with you.

2. **Aim for Simplicity and Clarity**

   A title should be easy to remember, ideally with just two or three words that are punchy yet meaningful. The best titles are often simple, direct, and memorable. The subtheme can provide more detail, giving readers a hint of what's inside without overwhelming them.

3. **Make It Reader-Centered**

   Imagine your title as a way to communicate directly with the reader you envisioned on Day 3. Choose words that speak to their journey, challenges, or aspirations. This connection is what will make them feel that your story has something valuable to offer them personally.

4. **Seek Feedback from Friends or Family**

    Once you have two or three potential titles and subthemes, ask people you trust for their impressions. Choose individuals who understand the purpose of your story or who are similar to your intended audience. Their feedback can help you gauge how the title might resonate beyond your perspective.

5. **Test the Emotional Impact**

    Ask yourself (and your feedback group): What emotion does this title evoke? Does it inspire curiosity, hope, or reflection? Choosing a title that connects emotionally will strengthen your story's appeal.

PROMPTS:

Use these prompts to brainstorm your book title and subtheme. Try to create a book title that is not more than three words. Your sub-theme can be a short sentence. Use this book's title as an example. Also, don't hesitate to look at other book covers to understand the impact of a short title and sub-theme.

- **Describe Your Core Message:** What is the main lesson or theme of your book in one or two sentences? How would you sum up the heart of your story?

- **Think of Your Ideal Reader:** What words or ideas would capture their attention? Imagine them seeing your book on a shelf—what would make them pick it up?

- **Identify Your Unique Voice:** What aspects of your journey or experiences set your story apart? Consider how a title might hint at these unique elements.

- **What Feelings Should the Title Evoke?** Do you want your title to inspire, challenge, confront, or comfort the reader? Identify the emotion you want the title to bring out in them.

- **What Words Reflect Your Transformation?** Consider words that symbolize your growth or key themes, like "overcoming," "journey," or "awakening." Are there any symbols or metaphors that come to mind?

EXPECTED RESULTS:

- A refined title of not more than three words that captures the essence of your story.

- A subtheme that adds depth, giving readers insight into what they can expect from your book.

- A list of 2-3 title options to test with friends or family for additional feedback.

A book's title bridges you and your reader. Create a title that's inviting, authentic, and reflective of your memoir's heart. Let it serve as both an invitation and a promise of the journey they'll embark upon with you.

DAY 22

GOAL: YOUR BOOK INTRODUCTION

This is the first time in this 30-day writing planner that your book's introduction is mentioned—and that was intentional. Here's why: crafting an introduction before knowing the full content of your book often results in a need for major revisions. By writing the introduction *after* completing your manuscript, you gain clarity on the themes, structure, and key messages of your manuscript. You now have a complete understanding of what your book represents and the journey it takes readers on.

Your book introduction is not just a formality; it's an essential tool to draw readers in. It sets the stage, piques curiosity, and invites them into your world. By this point, you've completed the bulk of your manuscript, so now it's time to focus on creating an introduction that aligns with your voice, themes, and the heart of your story.

This is your chance to captivate your audience, connect with their emotions, and encourage them to journey through the pages of your book. Your introduction should welcome readers, establish the tone, and provide a glimpse into the lessons, experiences, and truths you've shared. Let it be a reflection of your hard work and an open door to the powerful book you've written.

CRITERIA FOR WRITING YOUR INTRODUCTION:

1. **Start with a Hook**

   The opening of your introduction should grab attention. You might start with a vivid memory, an intriguing question, or a surprising statement that draws readers into your world. For example, you could begin with, "I never imagined I'd be telling this story," or "If you're holding this book, you might be searching for answers like I was." This sets a personal and engaging tone, inviting readers to step into your journey.

2. **Establish Your Purpose**

In the first few paragraphs, clarify why you wrote this memoir and what readers can expect. Explain your purpose openly: whether you hope to share lessons, provide inspiration, or simply tell the truth of your experiences. This will help readers understand the heart of your story and why it's worth their time.

3. **Introduce Key Themes**

Next, offer a glimpse of the main themes or struggles you'll explore in your book. Are you sharing a journey of overcoming adversity, finding faith, or reclaiming your voice? By introducing these themes early, you give readers a sense of the topics you'll cover, allowing them to connect more deeply with your story.

4. **Create a Personal Connection**

Use a conversational tone to speak directly to your ideal reader, making them feel seen and understood. Mention who this book is for—whether it's for someone seeking hope, healing, or insight. This personal touch can make readers feel that you're speaking directly to them, motivating them to read on with a sense of trust.

5. **End with an Intriguing Note**

Conclude your introduction by hinting at what lies ahead without revealing too much. Build a sense of curiosity that leads naturally into the first chapter. For example, you might say, "What I learned changed everything," or "I hope, by the end of this book, you'll find your own strength reflected here." This ending phrase invites readers to continue with a sense of anticipation.

TIME COMMITMENT:

30 minutes to 1 hour

PROMPTS:

Use these prompts to help you organize your introduction. Further, don't be afraid to write your ideas for each prompt on a separate document and create an outline or even several concepts of the flow of the introduction. Then, write the introduction. Essentially, the prompts are to gather your thoughts and then write your introduction.

- **Set the Scene:** What moment or idea will immediately capture your reader's attention? Consider starting with a powerful memory, question, or statement that draws readers in.

- **Explain Your Purpose:** Why did you write this memoir? What do you hope readers will gain from reading your story?

- **Highlight Key Themes:** Briefly touch on the main themes you'll explore in your book. What transformations, struggles, or lessons are central to your story?

- **Speak Directly to Your Reader:** Who is this book for? How does your story relate to them, and what do you want them to feel or understand by the end?

EXPECTED RESULTS:

- A well-organized introduction that engages readers and offers a clear glimpse into the journey they're about to embark on.

- A concise summary of the memoir's purpose and main themes, helping readers understand the value of your story.

- A compelling and authentic tone that resonates with the intended audience, motivating them to keep reading.

Writing your introduction after completing the book allows you to introduce your story with the full perspective of your journey. Make it genuine, purposeful, and reflective of the themes you've woven throughout, setting the perfect stage for the chapters to come.

"An introduction is the handshake between you and your reader; let it be warm, inviting, and full of promise for the journey ahead."

DAY 23

GOAL: CLOSING THOUGHTS

Not every single memoir requires having a closing chapter or what I like to call 'Closing Thoughts.' I always encouraged the author to step back from the completed work and decide if their script needs a closing (summary) chapter. So, this is what you will need to decide for yourself. Does your manuscript require a "Closing Thoughts?"

A final chapter is your opportunity to summarize your journey, reinforce the message, and leave a lasting impact on your readers.

CONCEPTS TO HELP DRAFT YOUR CLOSING THOUGHTS:

1. **Summarize Key Themes and Messages**

   Think about the central messages from each chapter. This final section is your chance to draw these together into one cohesive thread of thoughts, emphasizing how each experience contributed to your life.

2. **Highlight Your Transformation**

   Reflect on where you began and where you are now. This isn't just about detailing what happened but about capturing the deeper changes in your beliefs, understanding, and outlook. Show readers the journey of transformation.

3. **Reconnect to Your Purpose**

   Go back to your "why" from Day 1. Reaffirm your purpose in writing this memoir and how your story might help or inspire others on similar journeys. This closing chapter is your last chance to reinforce that purpose.

4. **Express Any Final Thoughts or Advice**

   If you have wisdom or insights that feel crucial, share them here. This is your last opportunity to speak directly to readers, guiding them toward the same resilience, hope, or understanding you've gained.

5. **End with a Note of Hope or Encouragement**

   A memoir's power often lies in its ability to inspire. Use your final words to leave readers with encouragement or hope, inviting them to reflect on their paths, empowered by the lessons you've shared.

TIME COMMITMENT:

45 minutes to 1 hour

PROMPTS:

Use the following prompts to help focus your closing thoughts and ensure you cover all key elements of your journey:

- **Reflect on Key Lessons:** What are the core lessons you've learned from the experiences you shared in each chapter? How have these lessons shaped you, and what do you want readers to remember most?

- **Summarize Your Transformation:** How have you changed from the person you were at the beginning to who you are now? Summarize your growth in a way that feels true and inspiring.

- **Tie Back to the Title and Subtheme:** How does your journey connect with your book's title and subtheme? Use your closing chapter to explain how these words reflect your life story's essence and purpose.

- **State Your Case:** What are the final thoughts you want to leave your readers with? Imagine this is your last opportunity to make your message clear. What truth or insight do you feel most compelled to share?

- **Express Gratitude and Hope:** Reflect on any gratitude you feel for those who played significant roles in your life, even if only briefly. How can you encourage your readers with hope, as they navigate their journeys?

EXPECTED RESULTS:

- A cohesive closing chapter that effectively summarizes the journey shared throughout your book.

- A clear, powerful statement of the main themes and lessons you've learned.

- A final, resonant connection between your life story, the title, and subtheme, leaving readers with a sense of closure and inspiration.

This final chapter is your closing message to your readers, a moment to encapsulate your story's heart and the legacy you wish to leave with them. Take the time to write from a place of honesty and depth, allowing your final thoughts to resonate.

So, now you must decide. Does your manuscript need 'Closing Thoughts?' The best way to decide is to look at the completed chapters, and if you believe you created a circle in your flow from chapter to chapter with your themes, you may not need one. But if you feel like the chapters need one more piece to connect everything together, then you likely may need to have a closing chapter.

"If you need Closing Thoughts, let it be the bridge to all your ideas as you leave the readers of your book inspired, motivated, or enthusiastic about your book, their success, and next steps."

Editing Days (Days 24-27)

Guidelines for Editing Days

Congratulations! You've completed your manuscript and entered the next critical phase of the journey: editing. Over the next few days, you'll embark on a self-editing phase, which involves refining your work to enhance clarity, polish, and flow. Self-editing differs from the professional edit your manuscript will later undergo; this is your chance to clean up your ideas, improve readability, and ensure the essence of your message shines through. Remember, your self-edit doesn't need to be perfect, but it will prepare your manuscript for the professional hands that will follow.

Goals for Self-Editing

Your focus during self-editing is to review three key areas: **line edits**, **grammar and spelling**, and **content flow**. Each of these will strengthen different aspects of your writing:

- **Line Edit:** A line edit involves examining each sentence to improve clarity, tone, and style. The goal is to ensure that each sentence contributes to your overall message and resonates with your voice. This may involve rephrasing awkward sentences, breaking up long paragraphs, or clarifying confusing ideas.

- **Grammar and Spelling Edit:** This stage is about catching grammatical errors, misspellings, punctuation mistakes, and other language details. It's essential for making your manuscript look polished and professional.

There are several free tools available to help with this aspect.

- **Content Flow Edit:** This focuses on the structure and readability of your manuscript. Review how each chapter connects, ensuring there is a logical progression. Look for any gaps or abrupt shifts that could disrupt the reader's experience. You want readers to feel like they're smoothly moving through your manuscript.

Differences Between Self-Editing and Professional Editing

Although the manuscript you have written is likely your first, I want to ensure that you fully comprehend the difference between Self-Editing and the Professional Editor.

While self-editing refines and clarifies your work, a professional editor brings an external perspective and expertise to take it further. Here's what to expect from an editor:

1. **Fresh Perspective**: Unlike you, an editor approaches your manuscript with fresh eyes. They're trained to spot areas where readers might struggle to understand or engage, making suggestions to clarify and enhance your writing.

2. **Enhanced Clarity and Consistency**: A professional editor will ensure your narrative flows smoothly and that your ideas are presented with clarity and consistency. They'll help refine your voice without changing your message, so readers connect with your story as you intended.

3. **Structural and Developmental Edits**: Beyond grammar and style, editors often provide feedback on the structure, pacing, and overall organization. They'll address any inconsistencies, flag unclear sections, and help highlight the strongest aspects of your story.

Using the Editing Articles

The daily articles in this section are meant to give you a deeper understanding of several aspects of the editing process. It's encouraged to treat each edit article as an individual process you perform on your manuscript. As you go along, you may begin to perform all of the aspects of editing at the same time. But if this is your first time writing a manuscript, it's best that you perform each edit aspect one at a time. So, it's important that you read each article and apply them. Use the articles as guides.

Remember: Self-editing is about making your manuscript as clear as possible from your perspective. Don't worry about perfection—this is your chance to polish your voice and message. When your manuscript reaches a professional editor, they'll help elevate your work, refining it further for a seamless, engaging reader experience.

DAY 24

GOAL: SPELLING

Today's focus is on one of the simplest yet most important aspects of editing: **spelling**.

Even if you were a spelling bee champion or pride yourself on your vocabulary, it's normal to misspell a word now and then. Thankfully, modern writing tools like Microsoft Word and Google Docs come equipped with built-in spell-check features that make this process much easier.

Your goal today is to ensure that your manuscript is free from spelling errors. A clean manuscript sets the tone for professionalism and clarity, making it easier for your future editor to focus on refining your story rather than catching basic mistakes.

Here are the steps to follow:

1. **Run a Spell Check:**

   Use the spell check feature in your writing software to identify and correct misspelled words. Pay attention to any flagged words that might be correctly spelled but used in the wrong context.

2. **Review Manually:**

   Don't rely solely on technology. Scan your manuscript to catch errors spell check might miss, such as homophones (e.g., "their" vs. "there").

3. **Focus on Accuracy Over Speed:**

   Take your time to ensure every chapter is reviewed thoroughly. This process might seem repetitive, but it's an essential step toward preparing your manuscript for publication.

4. **Spot Check for Consistency in Spelling Preferences:**
   If your manuscript uses terms that have alternate spellings (e.g., "color" vs. "colour" or "theater" vs. "theatre"), make sure they are consistent throughout. Decide on a preferred style based on your audience or regional norms and apply it uniformly across your work.

5. **Use a Dictionary or Thesaurus for Precision:**
   If you come across words you're unsure about, take a moment to look them up in a reliable dictionary. This not only helps confirm their spelling but ensures you're using the correct word for the context. Additionally, if a word feels repetitive, use a thesaurus to find alternatives that maintain the meaning without sounding redundant.

Time Commitment:

60 minutes to 2 hour

Prompts:

- Have I run a thorough spell check on my manuscript?

- Are there any words that could be clarified or improved for better readability?

- Have I double-checked names, places, and technical terms for accuracy?

Expected Results:

- A polished manuscript free from glaring spelling errors.

- Increased confidence in presenting your work to a professional editor.

- A strong foundation for the next stages of the editing process.

"Spelling may seem like a small detail, but it's the first step in transforming your manuscript into a polished and professional masterpiece."

DAY 25

GOAL: ADD DETAILS AND FIX GRAMMAR

Sometimes, you will read a part of your manuscript and say, "I forgot to add…" Then, sometimes you will read a part of your manuscript and say, "Did I share too much?" At this point in your writing journey, you are the only reader. Thus, it's sometimes difficult to know if you've shared enough information or not.

It's best to leave in the details you think are *too much*, and add the details in places where you think it's not enough. Remember, your goal with your manuscript is to capture your thoughts and content. When you work with your editor, they will ask you questions, or you can ask them questions to help you decide on the level of details you'd like to share.

Now when it comes to grammar, you may understand all of the rules of the English language, or you may struggle in this area. Thus, work with what you know. Don't put pressure on yourself if you're unsure. However, make updates based on what you understand. Once again, your editor will be a huge support with the grammar. So, don't overthink this aspect of editing. Simply do what you can, and the editor will work with you to enhance readability and clarity.

CONCEPTS TO HELP YOU ADD DETAILS AND FIX GRAMMAR:

1. **Focus on Adding Details**

   As you read through your manuscript, look for areas where additional details can enrich your manuscript. Ask yourself:

o   Are there moments where a reader might feel lost?

o   Have I described key settings, emotions, or actions vividly?

o   Could I include an example to make a point clearer?

Adding these details ensures your story is immersive and complete. Don't overthink it—write what feels natural, knowing that you can refine it later.

2. **Read Aloud for Flow and Clarity**

I do this all the time with manuscripts. I either read them aloud or use most writing software's "Read Aloud" feature.

Reading your manuscript aloud is a powerful way to identify awkward phrasing or sentences that don't flow well. Listen for areas where sentences feel clunky or repetitive and make adjustments as needed. This step also helps you identify where transitions between ideas might need strengthening.

3. **Keep Your Voice Front and Center**

While fixing grammar and adding details, remember to stay true to your natural voice. If a sentence feels too formal or rigid after a correction, adjust it to match your style. Readers are connecting with *you,* so ensure that your edits enhance—not diminish—your unique perspective.

4. **Save Major Changes for Your Editor**

    Avoid over-analyzing or rewriting large sections. Your editor will handle deeper edits, including sentence structure and grammar nuances. Thus, your edit focuses on cleaning up what you can and ensuring the manuscript reflects your intentions and ideas clearly.

5. ***Get Outta Your Head***

    I know the word *outta* isn't a real word. But look at how I presented it. I presented it in a manner to inform you, the reader, that there's something particular about the usage of this word. I kept it for the color that it adds.

    Some of the content you will write will require a similar style of presentation. While the writing may not be grammatically correct, the texture and color the words represent are understood.

    If you have areas of your manuscript that you're not sure of, Get *Outta* Your Head. As I stated, focus on your content. Write things how you think it should be written from a contextual and cultural stance. Add details and fix grammar based on what you know and not based on your uncertainty.

TIME COMMITMENT:

60 minutes to 2 hour

PROMPTS:

As you review your manuscript, use these questions to guide your process:

- **Do your sentences flow smoothly?** Read each paragraph to ensure it sounds natural and reflects your intended tone.

- **Are there areas where the details feel thin or rushed?** Look for moments where more description, context, or examples would enhance the reader's understanding or engagement.

- **Are there repetitive phrases or words?** Highlight and rephrase instances where repetition could distract readers or weaken your narrative.

- **Does the grammar align with your natural voice?** Remember, you're writing in your authentic voice, so ensure grammar supports clarity without altering your style.

- **Word Count Check** – Asses if your chapter is truly a chapter or is too long of a chapter. If you can't decide, definely have a conversation with your editor. They will support finalizing the decision.

EXPECTED RESULTS:

- A cleaner, more polished manuscript that reflects your best writing efforts.

- Enhanced descriptions and added details that improve the reader's experience.

- A foundation for the professional editing phase, with spelling and grammar errors minimized.

By addressing spelling, grammar, and content flow at this stage, you're preparing your manuscript to shine during the professional editing process. Take your time, stay consistent, and trust that each adjustment brings your story closer to its final form.

"Polishing your words is not about perfection—it's about making your voice shine brighter for readers to hear it clearly."

DAY 26

GOAL: FLOW OF CONTENT AND CONSISTENCY

In a court case, when the evidence is collected, and a timeline is prepared, it's used as a guide to confirm timelines associated with witnesses. This activity is what you will need to do with your manuscript.

Believe it or not, but sometimes you may have the timeline or other information incorrect. So, you have to ensure there's a logical flow of key details, such as dates, names, and timelines, that are consistent throughout. This will make your story easier to follow and more cohesive for readers.

CONCEPTS TO HELP YOU WITH THE FLOW OF CONTENT AND CONSISTENCY:

1. **Check the Logical Flow of Events**

   Read your manuscript chapter by chapter, asking yourself whether the sequence of events is logical. If something seems out of place, consider moving it to a different section. Think about the reader's experience—are you guiding them smoothly, or do they have to piece things together themselves? Adjust as necessary to ensure clarity.

2. **Review Timelines for Accuracy**

   Timelines are crucial in memoirs. Go through your manuscript and verify that dates, seasons, or periods align correctly with the events you're describing. Inconsistent timelines can confuse readers and distract from your narrative. If you're unsure of exact dates, use general terms (e.g., "early 1990s") to maintain consistency without being overly specific.

3. **Verify Names, Places, and Terminology**

   Ensure that names, locations, and specific terms are consistent throughout. For example, if you refer to someone as "Grandma" in one chapter, avoid switching to "Nana" or their full name unless it serves a purpose. Similarly, ensure place names or recurring phrases are spelled and formatted consistently.

4. **Strengthen Transitions**

   Transitions between sections or chapters should feel seamless. Check whether the end of one chapter flows naturally into the beginning of the next. If a transition feels abrupt, consider adding a sentence or two to bridge the gap. For example, you might reference a theme or foreshadow the next event to create continuity.

5. **Identify Repetition or Redundancy**

   Repetition can disrupt the flow of your story. Look for sections where you've repeated information unnecessarily and consolidate or remove it. Readers appreciate clarity and briefness, so avoid over-explaining points already covered.

TIME COMMITMENT:

60 minutes to 2 hour

PROMPTS:

Use these questions to guide your review of content flow and consistency:

- **Does the sequence of events make sense?** Are the chapters and sections in an order that naturally leads readers through your manuscript?

- **Are there any gaps in the timeline?** Do all key events have the necessary context, and are they placed chronologically (if applicable)?

- **Have you used consistent names and terminology?** Are people, places, and significant details referred to in the same way throughout the manuscript?

- **Do transitions between chapters and sections feel smooth?** Do they naturally guide the reader from one idea or event to the next?

EXPECTED RESULTS:

- A manuscript with a clear, logical structure that flows naturally from start to finish.

- Consistent use of names, dates, and other details, ensuring clarity for readers.

- Improved transitions between chapters and sections, creating a seamless reading experience.

By refining the flow and ensuring consistency in your manuscript, you create a smoother and more enjoyable experience for readers. Take your time with this review, keeping your audience in mind with every adjustment. A seamless, cohesive story is one of the greatest gifts you can offer your readers.

"A well-flowing story carries the reader effortlessly through the pages, leaving no room for confusion—only connection."

DAY 27

GOAL: FRESH EYES

This 30-Day challenge is meant to get you motivated and writing at a fast pace. You may have used some of the suggested time commitment, all of the suggested time commitment, or even more than the suggested time commitment. Regardless of your experience, this plan was meant to keep you moving. Thus, it's hard to have 'Fresh Eyes' when you're on the fast track. Let me explain.

'Fresh Eyes' is a perspective that requires you to review your manuscript as though you're encountering it for the first time. It forces you to read your manuscript as if you don't know what it's about. This action is hard to do with this 30-Day challenge, but you need to do it. Usually, I encourage aspiring authors to step away from their manuscript for at least three days and then use the fresh-eyes perspective. But you're on a journey. You're in a challenge. You must embark upon this task consciously and intentionally.

This step will help you identify areas that need improvement, ensure your narrative resonates with readers, and refine your work for clarity and engagement.

HOW TO USE FRESH-EYES:

1. **Take a Break Before Starting**

   Since this writing challenge is fast-paced, you have to perform 'fresh-eyes' by first mentally shutting down your thoughts. Your mental state needs to be objective. The goal is to create a sense of detachment, allowing you to read it not as the writer but as a first-time reader.

2. **Read It Aloud (Again)**

   Reading your manuscript aloud can help you experience its rhythm, tone, and pacing. This method often reveals awkward phrasing, abrupt transitions, or sentences that don't sound natural. Hearing the words spoken can also help you connect emotionally to your story, as a reader might.

3. **Mark Problem Areas**

   As you read, take notes or highlight sections that feel unclear, repetitive, or lacking in detail. Resist the urge to make edits immediately. Focus on understanding the reader's experience and jotting down your impressions. Edit the manuscript only after you finish completing 'fresh-eyes.'

4. **Focus on Reader Engagement**

   Ask yourself: Would this section hold my attention if I weren't the author? Are there moments where I'd feel emotionally invested, curious, or inspired? If any part feels flat or unengaging, consider how you can rework it to draw readers in.

5. **Check for Unanswered Questions**

   Readers often expect resolution or clarity by the end of a memoir. Look for areas where you may have unintentionally left questions unanswered or left readers wondering about details. Identify opportunities to provide closure or further context where necessary.

TIME COMMITMENT:

60 minutes to 2 hour

PROMPTS:

Use these questions to guide your "fresh eyes" review:

- **Does your story capture your attention as a reader?** Are there moments where your focus drifts, and how can you improve those sections?

- **Are your emotions conveyed clearly?** Do your words evoke the feelings and reactions you intended for your audience?

- **Are there areas where you feel lost or confused?** What details could help clarify or connect ideas?

- **Does the tone and voice remain consistent throughout the manuscript?**

- **What parts of the story stand out most?** Can you identify why they're compelling, and use that as inspiration to strengthen other areas?

EXPECTED RESULTS:

- A deeper understanding of how readers will experience your manuscript.

- Identification of areas needing improvement in terms of clarity, engagement, or tone.

- A more polished manuscript that resonates with your intended audience.

By reviewing your manuscript with fresh eyes, you'll uncover valuable insights about how your story will resonate with readers. This step is about shifting perspective—letting go of the role of the writer and fully embracing the role of the reader. With each adjustment, your manuscript will become more engaging, impactful, and ready for the next stage of its journey.

"To see your story with fresh eyes is to step into your readers' shoes—walking their path, feeling their emotions, and ensuring their journey is unforgettable."

Final Days (Days 28-30)

As you approach the final stretch of your 30-day writing journey, it's time to embrace the importance of finishing up. These last few days are not just about completing a task—they represent the culmination of your commitment, creativity, and perseverance. The manuscript you've crafted holds your story, your voice, and your truth. Now, it's time to bring it all together, ensuring your work is ready for the next stage of its journey.

Finishing up is a process of refinement and reflection. It's your opportunity to take a step back, see the bigger picture, and make any final adjustments. These days are about more than just writing—they're about honoring what you've accomplished and preparing to share your story with the world.

Remember, finishing doesn't mean achieving perfection. Your manuscript is a living document, and this phase is about giving it the shape and structure it needs to reflect your vision. It's about ensuring your thoughts are clear, your themes are consistent, and your message shines through. Finishing up is about giving yourself permission to say, "I've done the work, and I'm proud of what I've created."

Many aspiring authors who have worked with me have reached this point of their writing journey and felt the joy of almost having their manuscripts complete. It's like they were running a marathon and finally caught sight of the finish line. The sight of the end gave them the push to keep putting 'one foot in front of the other' to reach the finish line.

As you finish up, keep these thoughts in mind:

- **Stay Focused:** Use these final days to fully engage with your manuscript. Review it with intention and trust in the process you've followed.

- **Embrace Growth:** Recognize how far you've come, not just as a writer but as someone who dared to tell their story.

- **See the Bigger Picture:** This part of the writing journey resembles you pulling your head out of the dirt. Or coming up for air after an intense swim. The bigger picture of having a final manuscript takes center stage, which has your messages of truth.

- **Look Ahead:** This is the foundation of something greater. Finishing up doesn't mark the end; it's a powerful step toward sharing your voice with the world.

Take a deep breath and move forward with confidence. You've poured your heart into the pages of your manuscript, and now it's time to honor that effort by bringing your manuscript to completion. You're not just finishing up—you're preparing to take your story to the next level.

DAY 28

GOAL: REVIEWS AND REVISIONS

It's time to conduct a comprehensive review of your manuscript, focusing on a bird's eye view approach. Birds fly high in the sky and can see things at a level we humans cannot naturally see. Thus, we need to mentally take our minds to that of a bird during reviews and revisions.

The revisions you make here should be minor. It's about finalizing your voice, themes, and message before moving on to the final stages of the writing process.

STEPS TO YOUR REVIEW AND REVISION:

1. **Assess Content Flow and Structure**

   Look for sections where the flow could be improved. Ask yourself:

   o   Does each chapter build logically on the one before it?

   o   Are there paragraphs that would work better in a different section?

   o   Is there a natural progression from the beginning to the end of your manuscript?

   o   Make changes, if necessary.

   Complete this task from a conceptual viewpoint. Look at the Chapter titles and confirm that they flow from one thought to the next. Also, read sections of each chapter to assess the content flow and structure.

2. **Fine-Tune Your Voice and Tone**

Ensure that your voice is consistent throughout. Your tone should reflect your personality and the message you want to convey. If some sections feel too formal, too casual, or disconnected from the rest, revise them to match your intended style.

3. **Clarify Ambiguities**

Look for any sections where your meaning might not be clear to a reader. Add context, rephrase sentences, or expand on ideas to ensure your thoughts are fully understood. Remember, your readers won't have the same background knowledge as you, so clarity is key.

4. **Address Minor Revisions**

Make small adjustments to improve sentence structure, eliminate redundancy, and simplify complex phrasing. This is also a good time to catch any lingering spelling or grammar errors missed during earlier editing.

5. **Trust Your Judgment**

This is your story, told in your voice. As you review and revise, trust your instincts about what feels right and true to your journey. The goal is not to make your manuscript perfect but to ensure it represents you authentically and resonates with readers.

TIME COMMITMENT:

60 minutes to 2 hour

PROMPTS:

Use these questions to guide your review and revisions:

- **Does each chapter align with your intended themes?** Are the lessons and messages clear throughout your manuscript?

- **Are there any sections that feel out of place?** Would moving a paragraph or reordering content improve the flow?

- **Does the tone and voice remain consistent?** Is your authentic voice present in every chapter?

EXPECTED RESULTS:

- A refined manuscript that clearly conveys your message, themes, and intent.

- Improved flow and structure, ensuring a seamless reading experience.

- A near-final draft that reflects your voice and vision as an author.

What does your bird's eye view of your book tell you?

In the Foundational Days, you linked your events to your themes. But in *Reviews and Revisions*, you should be able to link your themes to your events. If you can readily do this, you've found a good balance between writing your life story in a manner that connects universally in themes and messages to an event that often varies from person to person. This is your bird's eye view.

"Revision is not about perfection—it's about ensuring your story feels true, clear, and uniquely yours."

DAY 29

GOAL: LET IT MARINATE

Take a step back and reflect on your manuscript as a whole, giving yourself permission to pause, relish your progress, and allow your work to settle before moving forward.

If you've ever marinated food, you know that sometimes the best flavors develop when you let the ingredients rest. The same applies to your manuscript. You've spent the last several weeks pouring your heart into your story, navigating milestones, reflecting on themes, and pushing through challenges. Now, it's time to let it marinate.

What does this mean?

Today, focus on the accomplishment of your journey rather than diving into intense edits or rewrites. You've already done the hard work—now is the moment to step back, breathe, and appreciate the incredible progress you've made. It's time to take an even bigger view higher than that associated with your bird's eye view.

IT'S TIME TO LET IT MARINATE:

1. **Spot-Check Sections**

   Choose a few random sections of your manuscript to read through. Even go to sections that are your favorite section. Don't analyze too deeply—just scan and let the words speak to you. How do they feel? Does the tone reflect what you intended? This is not a moment to fix things but to connect emotionally with what you've created.

2. **Relish the Accomplishment**

   As you review parts of your manuscript, take pride in what you've achieved. Whether it's one sentence that stands out, a powerful chapter, or the mere fact that you've written so much, allow yourself to feel the satisfaction of your progress.

3. **Avoid Overthinking**

   If you notice areas that feel incomplete or need improvement, resist the urge to dive in immediately. Acknowledge those sections but remind yourself: that's why editors exist. For now, focus on the bigger picture.

4. **Reconnect with Your "Why"**

   Revisit your original motivation for writing this book. How does the manuscript you've created so far align with that vision? Let the alignment—or even misalignment—settle in your mind without rushing to action.

5. **Pause and Trust the Process**

   This is your time to reflect, not revise. Trust that letting your work "sit" will help you approach it with fresher, clearer eyes when the time comes.

TIME COMMITMENT:

30 minutes to 2 hours

PROMPTS:

Use these questions to guide your reflection:

- What stands out to you as you read sections of your manuscript?

- How do you feel about the tone and flow of your work so far?

- Are there moments where your authentic voice shines through?

- How does it feel to see your story taking shape?

- Can you identify areas where you'll need an editor's help?

EXPECTED RESULTS:

- A renewed sense of accomplishment and confidence in what you've created.

- A deeper connection with your manuscript and its progress.

- An intentional pause that sets you up for stronger clarity and focus as you move forward.

By letting your manuscript marinate today, you're honoring the effort you've invested while preparing to approach the final steps. Celebrate your progress, reflect on your journey, and trust that the best is yet to come.

"Let your work rest for a moment—like marinated flavors, its essence will deepen with time."

DAY 30

GOAL: CELEBRATE AND REFLECT

It's time to *Celebrate* the incredible achievement of completing your writing journey over the past 30 days. Today is about recognizing the effort, commitment, and courage it took to write your manuscript and honoring the milestone you've reached.

CELEBRATE!

1. **Take Time to Reflect**

   Look back on the past 30 days and think about the challenges you faced, the breakthroughs you achieved, and the lessons you learned. Writing a book—especially your life story—is no small task. Reflecting on your journey will help you appreciate how far you've come.

2. **Celebrate Your Commitment**

   Many people dream of writing a book, but few ever begin. You didn't just start; you stayed committed for 30 days, and now you have a manuscript to show for it. Whether it took years to get to this point or just weeks, the fact that you followed through deserves celebration.

3. **Recognize the Achievement**

   Your manuscript may not feel "finished," but it's a monumental step toward completing your book. You've written down your ideas, told your story, and brought your voice to life. This is the foundation upon which your completed book will be built.

4. **Share Your Success**

   If you feel comfortable, share your accomplishment with someone you trust—whether it's a friend, family member, or mentor. Sharing your success not only validates your effort but can also inspire others to pursue their own goals.

5. **Look Ahead with Confidence**

   The next steps in the writing process—editing, revising, and publishing—are still ahead, but you've already proven your ability to commit and follow through. Trust in the foundation you've created and approach the next phases with the same dedication.

TIME COMMITMENT:

30 minutes (or as long as you need to celebrate!)

PROMPTS:

Use these prompts to guide your reflection and celebration:

- **How does it feel to have reached this point?** Reflect on your emotions now that you've completed the writing phase.

- **What challenges did you overcome during these 30 days?** Think about the moments of doubt, obstacles, or breakthroughs you experienced.

- **What are you most proud of?** Whether it's a specific chapter, a personal discovery, or simply sticking with the process, acknowledge your successes.

- **How has this process changed you?** Consider how writing your story has shaped your perspective, confidence, or connection to your purpose.

EXPECTED RESULTS:

- A sense of pride and accomplishment for completing your manuscript, regardless of how "complete" it feels.

- A deeper appreciation for the commitment and effort you invested in this process.

- Renewed motivation and excitement for the next stages of your journey as an author.

Today, honor the work you've done and the courage it took to tell your story. You've achieved something remarkable in these 30 days, and your story is ready to move into the next chapter of its journey. Celebrate, reflect, and know that you've already succeeded by simply showing up and writing.

"You wrote the story only you could tell, and in doing so, you've accomplished what so many only dream of. Celebrate this moment—it's the foundation of something extraordinary."

Next Steps

Release Your Book to the World

As you reach the end of this 30-day journey, you've accomplished something remarkable—you've written your manuscript. Take a moment to reflect on the transformation you've experienced over the past month. The doubts, the hesitation, and the years of uncertainty have been replaced with a manuscript that holds your story, your voice, and your truth. You've done what many only dream of, and now, it's time to move into the next chapter of your journey.

So, what comes next?

You're standing at another pivotal crossroads. The door to your left says, "Wait and see." The door to your right says, "Take the next step." The decision is yours, but let me remind you: momentum is everything. The commitment and drive that got you here must carry you forward. Don't let hesitation creep in. You've come too far to stop now.

The next phase is about preparing your manuscript for the world to read. This is where professional editing, cover design, and publication come into play. These steps are vital to transforming your manuscript into a polished, impactful book that will resonate with readers and leave a lasting impression.

The Importance of the Next Steps

Your manuscript represents the heart of your story, but the next steps will ensure that story is polished and ready to shine. A professional editor will refine your words, clarify your ideas, and help your book flow seamlessly. A well-designed cover will grab the attention of readers, and the right publication strategy will place your book in their hands. These steps take your vision and make it a reality.

But these steps don't happen on their own. They require action. They require commitment. They require the same dedication that carried you through the past 30 days.

Why Keep the Momentum?

Many aspiring authors stop at this point, overwhelmed by the next phase. They set their manuscripts aside, promising themselves they'll come back to it later. Months, even years, pass, and their stories remain untold. Don't let that be your story. Keep the momentum. Keep moving forward.

Your Call to Action

I'm here to help you take those next steps. As your writing coach, I've guided you through the process of getting your story onto the page, and now I can help you turn that story into a published book. Together, we can navigate the editing process, create a captivating cover, and plan a publication strategy that ensures your book reaches its intended audience.

Imagine this: In six months, you're holding your book in your hands. It's sitting on shelves, available for readers who need the message only you can deliver. Your journey from idea to impact will be complete. But it all starts here—with your decision to take action.

Here's what you need to do next:

- **Contact me today:** Let's discuss the steps to move your book from manuscript to masterpiece.

- **Book a strategy session:** Together, we'll map out the path of your next steps.

- **Email or call:** Take the first step toward seeing your story in print.

Website: www.CoachVarKelly.com | www.JustWriteItServices.com

Email: Info@JustWriteItServices.com

Phone: (803) 274-2155

The hardest part—writing your story—is behind you. Now, it's time to honor that effort by taking the next steps. Don't let this moment pass you by. You've done the work; you've told your story. Now, let's release it to the world. **The door is open—are you ready to walk through?**

ABOUT THE AUTHOR

Var Kelly, the youngest of four children and the son of Mary Kelly and the late Ivory Kelly, is a celebrated writing coach, author, and mentor. Despite early struggles with reading, writing, and phonics, Var's journey is a testament to perseverance. He overcame these challenges through determination, eventually earning a bachelor's degree and a Doctorate. He has excelled as an analytical chemist and scientist, and he has even managed research and development.

Yet, Var's life took an extraordinary turn when his analytical expertise intertwined with his faith, leading him to author his first book, *The Faith Reaction,* in 2010. That experience ignited a passion for writing and mentoring others, ultimately shaping his mission: to empower individuals to transform their stories into tools of healing, growth, and legacy.

As a professional writing coach with over 20 years of experience, Var has guided countless aspiring authors to overcome writing hurdles, organize their thoughts, and complete manuscripts they once thought impossible. He customizes his programs to meet clients where they are, drawing on his unique ability to make the writing process accessible, engaging, and transformative.

Var's latest work, *Write Your Book: A 30-Day Writing Guide to Sharing Your Story with the World,* exemplifies his dedication to helping individuals—especially individuals balancing family, careers, businesses, and personal dreams—tell their stories with confidence.

Through his faith, personal growth, and a deep connection to his clients, Var Kelly continues to inspire others to move from tragedy to triumph, from a story untold to a legacy that impacts generations.

THANK YOU FOR READING!

I hope this book has blessed you, inspired you, and impacted your life. Your feedback is incredibly important, and I'd love to hear from you!

Leave a Review and 5-Star Rating

How to Leave a Review on Amazon

1. Go to the book's page on **Amazon** (search for the title or author).

2. Scroll down to the **Customer Reviews** section.

3. Click on **"Write a Customer Review."**

4. Select the number of stars and write your feedback.

5. Click **Submit**—and that's it!

Thank you for your support. Your feedback can help others find this book and experience the same impact.

May GOD continue to bless and guide you on your journey.

www.ingramcontent.com/pod-product-compliance
Lightning Source LLC
Chambersburg PA
CBHW061658120626

46550CB00003B/999

* 9 7 9 8 9 9 2 6 5 8 6 8 2 *